UP CLOSE

SEA SWIMMERS

A CLOSE-UP PHOTOGRAPHIC LOOK INSIDE YOUR WORLD

Written by Heidi Fiedler

Quarto Library

This library edition published in 2017 by Walter Foster Jr.,
an imprint of The Quarto Group
6 Orchard Road, Suite 100
Lake Forest, CA 92630

Project Editor: Heidi Fiedler
Written by Heidi Fiedler
Cover photography by Audrey Narchuk.
Photographs on pages 7 (center), 14, and 18–20 by Alexander Semenov.
Photograph on page 8 by Todd Winner.
Photographs on pages 6 (top) and 16 by Audrey Narchuk.
Photographs on pages 24–25 by Linden Gledhill.
Photographs on pages 26 and 28 by Henry Jager.
All other images © Shutterstock.

Distributed in the United States and Canada by
Lerner Publisher Services
241 First Avenue North
Minneapolis, MN 55401 U.S.A.
www.lernerbooks.com

First Library Edition

Library of Congress Cataloging-in-Publication Data

Names: Fiedler, Heidi, author.
Title: Sea swimmers : a close-up photographic look inside your world / written by Heidi Fiedler.
Description: First library edition. | Lake Forest, CA : Walter Foster Publishing, 2017. | Audience: Ages 8+. | Includes bibliographical references and index.
Identifiers: LCCN 2017011688 | ISBN 9781942875345 (hardcover : alk. paper)
Subjects: LCSH: Marine animals--Juvenile literature. | Marine fishes--Juvenile literature. | Photography, Close-up--Juvenile literature.
Classification: LCC QL122.2 .F54 2017 | DDC 591.77--dc23
LC record available at https://lccn.loc.gov/2017011688

Printed in USA
9 8 7 6 5 4 3 2 1

MIX
Paper from responsible sources
FSC® C008080
www.fsc.org

Are You Ready for Your Close-up?

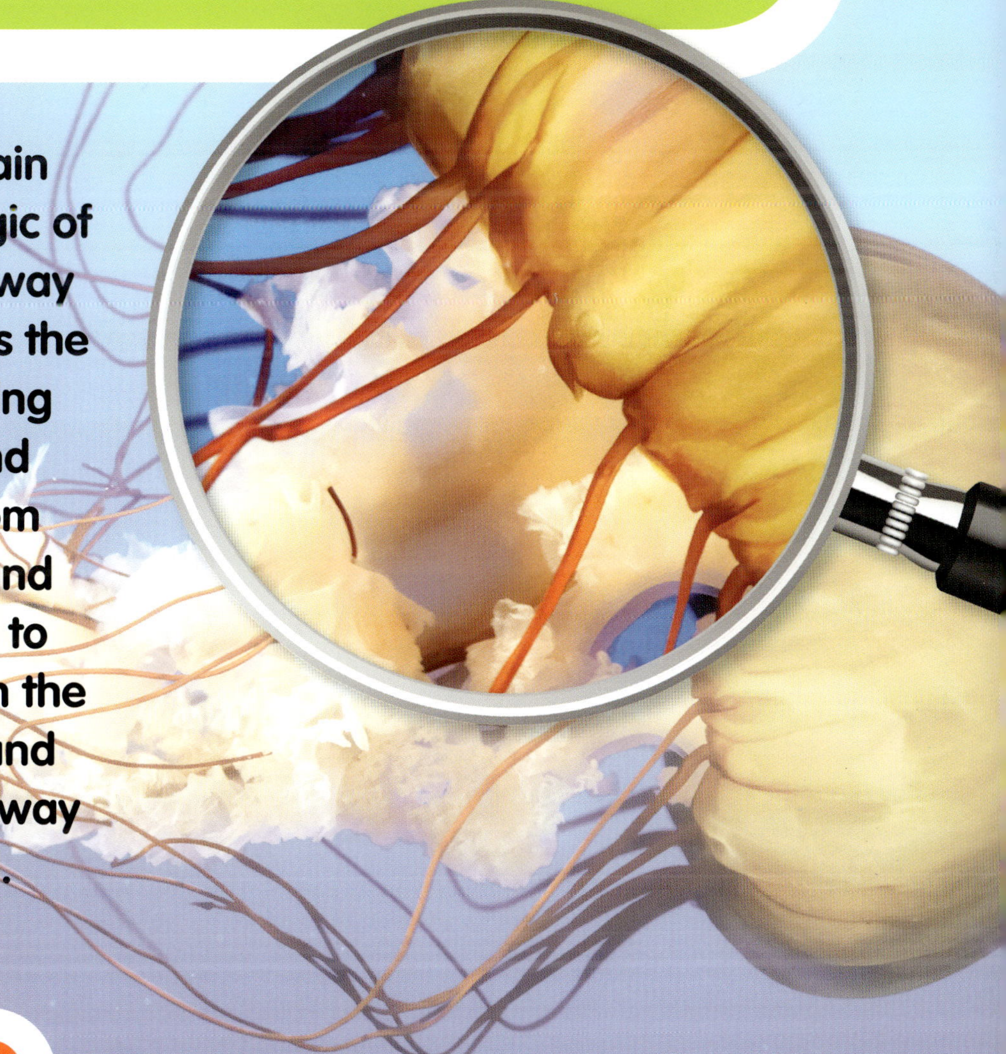

Can you feel your brain tickling? That's the magic of looking at something way UP CLOSE. It transforms the ordinary into something new and strange and inspires everyone from hi-tech shutterbugs and supersmart scientists to look again. So let's turn the ZOOM up to eleven and discover a whole new way of seeing the world.

How Eye See the World

"Whatcha lookin' at?" That's the question people have been asking each other for thousands of years. The first humans observed interesting—and important—things like woolly mammoths, lightning, and each other. Early artists moved on to painting and drawing what they saw. Finally, in 1862, photography allowed people to capture what they saw in new and amazing ways.

Today, photographs are everywhere. Cereal boxes, bulletin boards, and T-shirts are all home to photos. A simple image search online can produce cootchie-cootchie-coo images of bright-eyed babies or stark, white, snowy landscapes. Photographers capture everything from moments of joy and pain to the wonders that exist in the cracks and hidden layers of our busy world. They focus their attention on a huge range of subjects, and the images they produce reveal how everyone sees the world in their own unique way.

The History of Photography

Black-and-White Photography

1826
Nicéphore Niépce creates the first photograph. It takes 8 hours.

1859
Photography goes panoramic.

1839
Daguerreotypes capture rough images on pieces of metal.

1877
Eadweard Muybridge invents a way to shoot objects—such as horses—in motion.

Color Photography

1888
Kodak™ produces the first mass-produced camera.

1912
The 35mm camera takes center stage.

1930
Flash bulbs help photographers capture images in low light.

1935
New techniques make color photography shine.

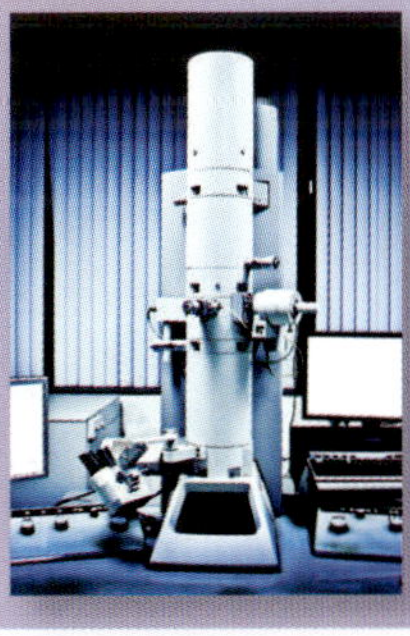

1939
An electron microscope reveals what a virus looks like.

1946
Zoomar produces the zoom lens.

Digital Photography

1976
Canon® produces the first camera with a microprocessor.

"**Photography**...has **little** to do with the things you **see** and **everything** to do with the **way** you **see** them."
—Elliott Erwitt

1992
The first JPEG is produced.

2015
Instagram is home to more than 20 billion images.

Extreme Close-up!

Photography has been helping people express how they see the world for nearly 200 years, and in that time, things have gone way beyond taking a simple shot of a horse or a sunset. Today, photographers are pushing the limits of technology.

Macro photographers use large lenses to get WAY up close to their subjects. They can magnify an object to more than five times its size, using special lenses that reveal patterns and textures that wow viewers.

Coleman shrimp

Micro photography goes even further. It uses a microscope to reveal details humans could never see before. It can make a diatom look like a glowing planet or a priceless piece of jewelry.

The deep blue oceans of our planet are some of the last places on Earth that have yet to be explored. And photographers are leading the way. Some are scientists, studying creatures that have no names. Others simply love being underwater, where life is more colorful and stranger than we could ever imagine. Take a look!

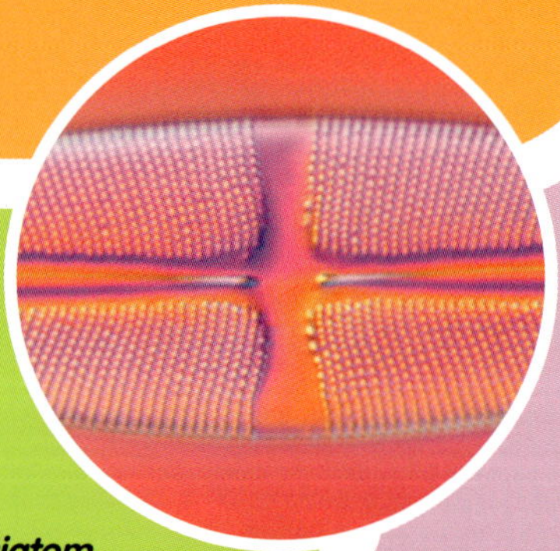

Diatom

Getting the Shot

Photographers choose where and how they want to work based on what type of images they want to produce.

European chub scales

Out in the Field

Macro photographers can take their giant lenses underwater to capture sea life in its natural environment.

King ragworm

In the Studio

Working inside lets photographers have more control over the lighting, the angle of the camera, and their subject.

Water flea

Under the Microscope

A microscope allows photographers to look at their subjects in even more detail.

The Abyss

Down,
Down,
Down,
It goes.
Where it stops,
No one knows.
Lost in an underwater maze.
There's no map. Just haze.

Bird's Eye View

But up, up, up…and the abyss is transformed. With a hard, beak-like mouth and colorful scales, the parrotfish is easy to recognize. Welcome to the jungle.

Pajama Party

At night, parrotfish produce a layer of mucus around their heads. But this isn't just a soft pillow to rest on. Experts think the mucus masks the fish's smell, which makes it less likely to be eaten while it sleeps.

Scientific Name: Scaridae
Size: 1 to 4 feet long
Habitat: Coral reefs around the world
Diet: Algae and coral

Some have called the parrotfish the most colorful fish in the world.

Mosaic jellyfish

A Big (Beautiful) Blob

The great explorers of the world travel by foot, on trains, and up above our heads in planes. But jellyfish float. And their movements are mesmerizing. Jellyfish come in all shapes and sizes, and their names are just as strange. There's egg-yolk jellyfish, blubber jelly, hair, moon, mosaic, and more.

Scientific Name: There are more than 200 types of jellies
Size: Can range between 1 and 75 inches
Habitat: Around the world
Diet: Tiny crustaceans, small fish, plankton, and other jellyfish

Many lion's mane jellies are bioluminescent and act as their own flashlight in the deep dark waters of the sea.

Tangled Tentacles

If you think it's hard to untangle the wires on your earphones, try keeping a zillion tentacles straight. Jellyfish don't seem to mind when they get a snarl in their "hair." As long as they can glide through the water, they'll keep swimming. If they're not careful, smaller jellies can get caught in a larger jellyfish's tentacles too. In an aquarium, scientists use a glass rod to help untie the knot, if needed.

Atlantic sea nettle

The ocean shall be mine! Muahhahaha!

Creatures great and small make their home in the ocean. This crustacean is about the size of your thumb, but it makes a big impact. Hundreds of marine animals depend on zooplankton for food. These little guys also know how to travel in style. They hitch a ride under the bells of jellyfish and make themselves at home, feasting on jellyfish eggs and whatever the jellyfish eats.

Scientific Name: Hyperia galba
Size: .5 to 1 inch long
Habitat: Inside jellyfish in North Atlantic and Pacific Oceans
Diet: Jellyfish eggs and the food eaten by jellyfish

Crustaceans are sometimes called "underwater bugs" because, like insects, they belong to the Arthropoda phylum.

Crusty Creatures

Crustaceans have hard shells and lots of legs. They include everything from crabs to lobsters—and Hyperia galbas.

Hide and Seek

Coleman shrimp sightings are rare—maybe because they know just how to blend in. The red-and-white Coleman shrimp lives on the fire urchin, which is known for its toxic touch. But this species has developed the ability to survive the urchin's painful stingers.

Scientific Name: Periclimenes colemani
Size: Less than an inch long
Habitat: Deep off of the coast of Indonesia
Diet: Algae and plankton

"What is a scientist after all? It is a curious man looking through a keyhole, the keyhole of nature, trying to know what's going on."
–Jacques Cousteau

Masters of Disguise

Many animals use camouflage to blend in and hide from predators. Some change their colors or their shape. Others find a safe place to hide or look more intimidating than they actually are.

Somewhere Over the Rainbow

Legs shine bright...
There are so many legs.
Too many to count.
At night.

King of the Worms

Meet the creepiest, crawliest critter of the deep: King Ragworm. Like all annelid worms, it has a segmented body, movable bristles, and a long body cavity. Many, like this one, have a disturbing number of legs. And most can regrow their tails! It may be marine royalty, but the king ragworm spends much of its time burrowed in sand and mud. Don't underestimate it though. When it's time to defend its territory, it won't hesitate to bite or thrash about violently. A nasty fight can end with one or more worms in a knot.

Scientific Name:
Alitta virens
Size: Up to 47 inches long
Habitat: Northern Hemisphere
Diet: Carrion, small fish, crustaceans, and mollusks

This worm's "legs" are actually parapodia, which act both as legs and gills.

Sound the Alarm!

When they're competing for resources, king ragworms go to war with each other, but like frenemies, they also depend on each other. They look to each other to detect traces of ragworms that have been eaten or left behind in the water by a predator after an attack. At the first sign of dead ragworms, one ragworm sounds the alarm and the others head for safety.

An Angry Clown

What kind of clown can't turn a smile upside down? A clownfish! The good news is that with their bright white stripes, clownfish are as easy to spot as a clown wearing a big red nose.

Scientific Name: Amphiprion percula
Size: 2 to 5 inches long
Habitat: Indian and Pacific Oceans
Diet: Other small fish

Scientists think the moonlight on extra bright nights helps clownfish know when it's time to mate.

Queen of the Clowns

Clownfish live in groups, with one female and up to five males. The female is always the largest in the group.

Diving Deep

Microscopic photography is revealing thousands of creatures we never knew existed. Diatoms are very simple creatures, but the shapes they take vary nearly as much as snowflakes. Some are round and barely move. Others are long and glide through the water. They're found around the world in mud, water—and the stomachs of the many animals that eat them.

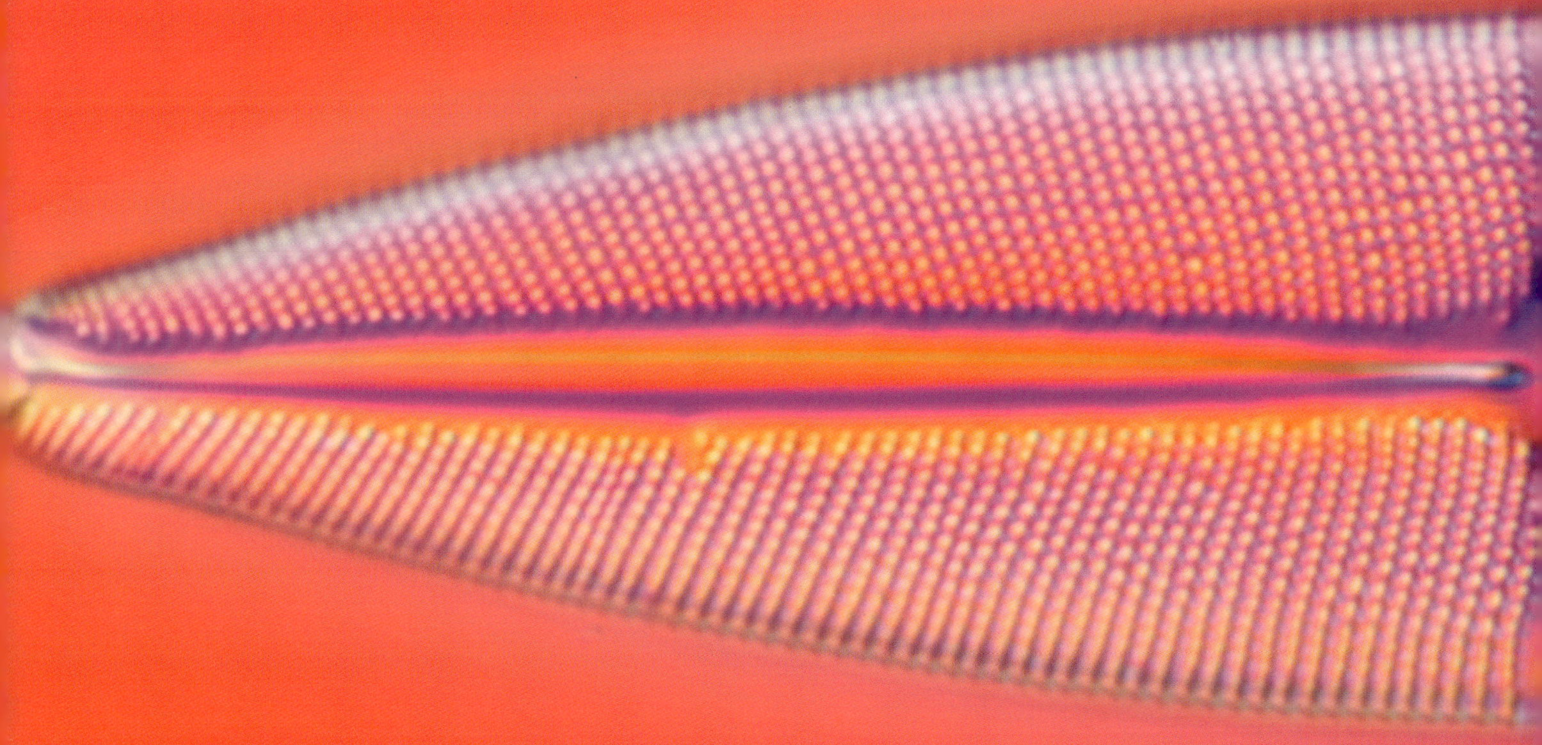

Each **diatom** is **surrounded** by a thin wall of **silica**–the same compound that makes up **glass**.

Scientific Name: Scientists have identified 16,000 different species of diatoms!
Size: Single-celled
Habitat: Pretty much anywhere that's wet
Diet: Most make their own food in the same way plants do

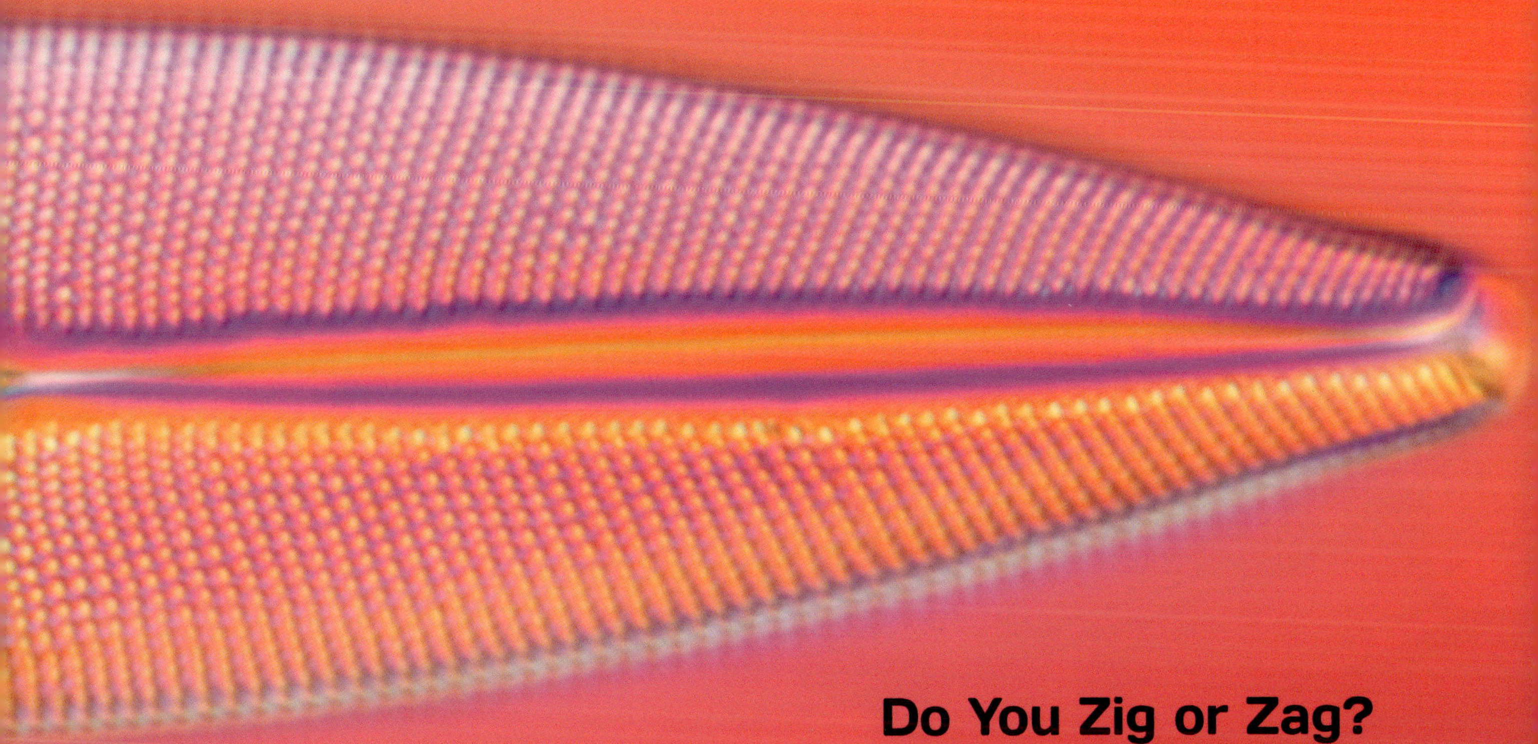

Do You Zig or Zag?

Some diatoms float through the world all alone. But others live in colonies. Together they can form strange ribbon, fan, zigzag, or star shapes.

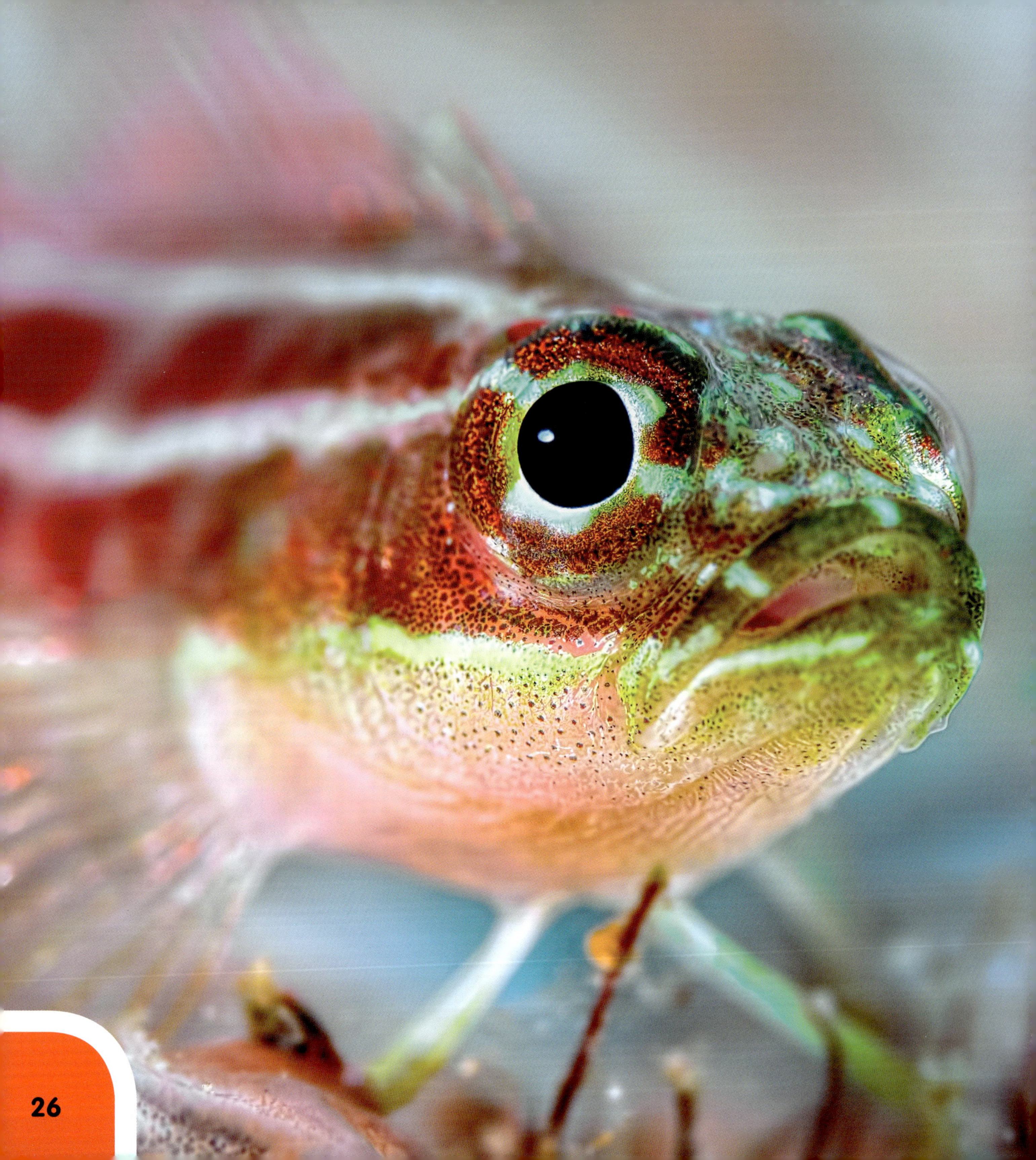

Glub. Glub. Grub.

A day in the life of a goby fish is filled with swimming and eating. It relies on its wide mouth to eat, build a home, and get where it wants to go. A Hawaiian goby species has even found a way to use its mouth as a suction cup to climb up the 300-foot-tall waterfalls it lives in. Gobies come in a rainbow of colors. They're often found burrowing in sand or mud. They come out to feed, but when it's time to stay home, they use their fins as suctions to grab hold of rocks and stay secure.

Only the Best for My Little Goby

To make sure the world always has more gobies, these fish lay eggs, attach them to a shell or rock, and then the males guard them carefully. Well, kind of. They guard the eggs whenever the female gobies are watching. But otherwise, they're off duty.

Scientific Name: Gobiidae
Size: 2 to 20 inches
Habitat: Throughout the world, most often in the tropics
Diet: Meat eaters, many act as parasites, feeding from the bodies of larger fish

Some gobies share homes with burrowing worms, pea crabs, or snapping shrimp.

Underwater Pixies

Itty-bitty, teeny-tiny pygmy seahorses use camouflage to hide from predators. They live on coral sea fans that hide them perfectly. Baby pygmies are born a dull brown color, but they change color to match their home. Pygmies born on orange sea fans become orange. And pygmies born on purple sea fans become purple. They grow bumps to match the texture of the sea fans. Then they hook their tails around a branch and settle in, safe from the ocean's currents.

Scientific Name: Hippocampus bargibanti
Size: Less than an inch tall
Habitat: Corals in tropical waters
Diet: Small crustaceans

Each morning, pygmy seahorses greet their mates with a special dance that includes rubbing snouts.

You Are Now Entering The Twilight Zone

Pygmy seahorses live in a mysterious layer of the ocean called "The Twilight Zone." Sunlight rarely reaches this area, and little is known about it.

Behind the Lens

Now it's your turn! Grab a camera and start shooting whenever you see something that amazes you or makes you curious to learn more. If you want to go macro without spending too much money, snap a macro lens band over a cellphone camera. Whatever camera you use, these tips will help you get started.

The flash lights the subject.

The shutter acts like a camera, opening and closing to let light into the camera for short periods of time.

The lens is the curved piece of glass that light travels through before reaching a sensor or film inside the camera.

A tripod keeps the camera steady.

The size of the opening in the lens is the aperture. It's measured in fractions.

The focal point is the part of the image that's sharp.

The depth of field is the distance between the parts of an object that are in focus. In micro and macro photography, this distance is very small.

Some lenses have a short focal length and produce a wider angle of view. Other lenses have a longer focal length.

Aperture Scale

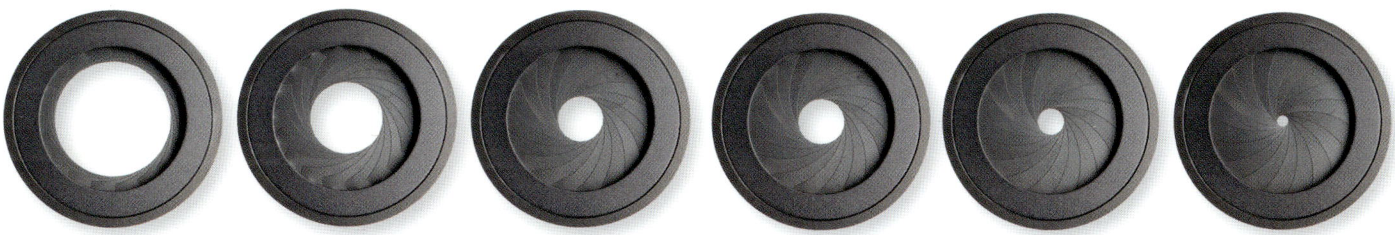

f/1.4 f/2.8 f/5.6 f/8 f/16 f/22

Large aperture ↔ Small aperture

More light strikes image sensor ↔ Less light strikes image sensor

Shallow Depth of Field (Focus) ↔ Deep Depth of Field (Focus)

Index

Clownfish, *Amphiprion percula* 22–23

Crustacean, *Hyperia galba* 14–15

Crustacean, Coleman Shrimp,
Periclimenes colemani 6, 16–17

Diatom 24–25

Fish scales, European chub, *Leuciscus cephalus* 7

Goby fish, *Gobiidae* 26–27

Jellyfish, *Mosaic* 12

Jellyfish, Atlantic sea nettle 3, 13

King ragworm, *Alitta virens* 7, 18–21

Parrotfish, *Scaridae* 8, 10–11

Seahorse, pygmy, *Hippocampus bargibanti* 28–29

Water flea, *Daphnia ambigua* 7